The
LOVE
BETWEEN
Mother
AND
Daughter
IS
FOREVER

A WARM THANK YOU!

Dear Reader,
By choosing this journal, you're nurturing a deeper bond with your daughter. This is not just a book—it's a vessel for heartfelt communication, growth, and love. I've passionately poured my heart and soul into each page, and knowing it's found a home in your hands fills me with immense joy and gratitude. I feel humbled and honored to be a part of your story.

As an independent author, I've drawn from my own life experiences to create this tool. My aim? To support families like yours and foster the development of confident, strong women.

YOUR OPINION MATTERS IMMENSELY

Your voice is essential to me. Honest reviews on Amazon do more than increase my visibility—they offer invaluable insights that help me improve. If this journal serves you well, I'd be grateful for an honest review. Your support empowers me to continue crafting tools that help families grow closer.

I'M COMMITTED TO YOUR SATISFACTION

Despite my best efforts to ensure perfection, occasional printing errors can occur. If you come across any flaws, please contact the place of purchase for a replacement. I deeply value your satisfaction and understanding, and I hope you can extend some grace for those out-of-control instances.

In closing, I want to express my heartfelt gratitude for joining me on this exciting journey. Your decision to use this journal makes you a part of my own unique story, a privilege that I deeply cherish.

Best wishes,

Brit A. Anderson

THIS JOURNAL BELONGS TO...

AND

DATE:

THE
JOURNEY

Take your time. This isn't a race and no one is taking score of how and when you fill out this book.

HOW IT WORKS

THIS SHOULD BE SOMETHING FUN TO DO TOGETHER

You don't have to fill out every question.
You don't have to go in order.
There is no time limit to answering the questions.
Use it as a tool for school projects.
Write as much or as a little as you want.

DON'T BE AFRAID TO LET IT ALL OUT. LEARN ABOUT EACH OTHER AND YOURSELF.

This book was created to help connect and grow the bond between a Mother and Daughter. It can also help build writing skills and open lines of communication, to help express feelings that may be hard to talk about.

IT ALSO MAKES FOR A GREAT KEEPSAKE TO LOOK BACK ON IN FUTURE YEARS.

HAVE FUN!....

I am, who I am

In this section, talk a bit about you.
How was it growing up as a kid, Mom?
Daughter, how is it being a kid and growing
up with Mom?

ONCE YOU HAVE COMPLETED THIS SECTION,
DISCUSS SOME THINGS YOU LEARNED ABOUT
EACH OTHER THAT YOU DIDN'T KNOW BEFORE.

WHAT IT'S LIKE BEING ME...

MY FULL NAME IS... .... I AM .... YEARS OLD.

WERE YOU NAMED AFTER SOMEONE? ....

I WAS BORN IN... .... I CURRENTLY LIVE IN... ....

I HAVE MOVED .... TIMES IN MY LIFE.

MY FAVORITE THING TO DO NOW IS... ....
....

MY FAVORITE THING TO DO WHEN I WAS YOUNGER WAS... ....
....
....

AS A KID I DREAMED OF BEING .... WHEN I GREW UP.

MY CURRENT OCCUPATION IS... ....

MY FAVORITE THING ABOUT ME IS ....
....
....

MY LEAST FAVORITE THING ABOUT ME IS ....
....

I AM MOST AFRAID OF... ....

MY WORST HABIT IS ....

I HAVE .... SIBLINGS.

WHAT DID YOU LIKE MOST ABOUT HAVING SIBLINGS? OR BEING AN ONLY CHILD?
....
....

MY FULL NAME IS...   I AM   YEARS OLD.

WERE YOU NAMED AFTER SOMEONE?

I WAS BORN IN...   I CURRENTLY LIVE IN...

I HAVE MOVED   TIMES IN MY LIFE.

MY FAVORITE THING TO DO NOW IS...

MY LEAST FAVORITE THING TO DO NOW IS...

I DREAM OF BEING A   WHEN I AM OLDER.

MY FAVORITE THING ABOUT ME IS

MY LEAST FAVORITE THING ABOUT ME IS

I AM MOST AFRAID OF...

MY WORST HABIT IS

I HAVE   SIBLINGS.

WHAT DO YOU LIKE MOST ABOUT HAVING SIBLINGS? OR BEING AN ONLY CHILD?

Favorites!

Each of you fill out this section with all
your favorite things!
Are you surprised by ones you didn't
know about before?

**THEN GO BACK AND COMPARE
TO SEE HOW MANY YOU HAVE IN COMMON.**

FILL THESE OUT AND HAVE FUN!

DONUT

BREAKFAST

CHIPS

FRUIT

SNACK

CRACKERS

CEREAL

CANDY

Mom's FAVORITE THINGS!

LUNCH

RESTAURANT

DRINK

CAKE/PIE

DINNER

PASTA

COOKIE

DESSERT

VEGETABLE

PIZZA TOPPING

ICE CREAM

YAY!!

11

FILL THESE OUT AND HAVE FUN!

DONUT

FRUIT

CEREAL

BREAKFAST

CHIPS

SNACK

CRACKERS

CANDY

LUNCH

Daughter's FAVORITE THINGS!

DRINK

RESTAURANT

CAKE/PIE

DINNER

PASTA

COOKIE

DESSERT

VEGETABLE

PIZZA TOPPING

ICE CREAM

YAY!!

FILL THESE OUT AND HAVE FUN!

SPORT TO PLAY

HOBBY

SPORT TO WATCH

SPORTS TEAM

SMELL

COLOR

SOUND

PATTERN

ANIMAL

STORE

NUMBER

Mom's FAVORITE THINGS!

TYPE OF WEATHER

MONTH

CITY

STATE

DAY OF WEEK

TIME OF DAY

VACATION SPOT

COUNTRY

YAY!!

FILL THESE OUT AND HAVE FUN!

SPORT TO PLAY

HOBBY

SPORT TO WATCH

SPORTS TEAM

SMELL

COLOR

SOUND

PATTERN

ANIMAL

Daughter's FAVORITE THINGS!

STORE

NUMBER

STATE

TYPE OF WEATHER

MONTH

CITY

COUNTRY

DAY OF WEEK

TIME OF DAY

VACATION SPOT

YAY!!

FILL THESE OUT AND HAVE FUN!

ACTRESS

MOVIE

MUSIC GENRE

ACTOR

BAND

SINGER

COMEDIAN

SONG

BOOK

Mom's FAVORITE THINGS!

PODCAST

PHONE APP

YOUTUBE

AMUSEMENT PARK

SEASON

BOARD GAME

TV SHOW

LAKE

BEACH

CARTOON

YAY!!

ACTRESS

MOVIE

MUSIC GENRE

ACTOR

BAND

SINGER

COMEDIAN

SONG

BOOK

Daughter's FAVORITE THINGS!

PODCAST

PHONE APP

YOUTUBE

AMUSEMENT PARK

SEASON

BOARD GAME

TV SHOW

LAKE

BEACH

CARTOON

YAY!!

Hypotheticals

Use your imagination and explore these hypothetical situations. Feel free to skip around or do them in order.

DISCUSS WHAT YOU WROTE AND COMPARE YOUR SIMILARITIES AND DIFFERENCES.

YOU HAVE BUILT A TIME MACHINE...

MOM, FILL OUT THIS SCENARIO

☐ PAST	☐ FUTURE

WHERE DO YOU WANT TO GO?

WHY DID YOU CHOOSE THIS TIME?

WILL YOU TAKE ANYONE WITH YOU? IF SO, WHO?	HOW LONG DO YOU WANT TO STAY?

WHO DO YOU WANT TO MEET?

IF YOU COULD CHANGE ONE THING IN THIS TIME WITHOUT CONSEQUENCES, WHAT WOULD IT BE?

YOU HAVE BUILT A TIME MACHINE...

DAUGHTER, FILL OUT THIS SCENARIO

❑ **PAST**   ❑ **FUTURE**

WHERE DO YOU WANT TO GO?

_____

_____

WHY DID YOU CHOOSE THIS TIME?

_____

_____

_____

WILL YOU TAKE ANYONE WITH YOU? IF SO, WHO?	HOW LONG DO YOU WANT TO STAY?

WHO DO YOU WANT TO MEET?

_____

_____

_____

IF YOU COULD CHANGE ONE THING IN THIS TIME WITHOUT CONSEQUENCES, WHAT WOULD IT BE?

_____

_____

_____

YOU HAVE AN EMPTY ROOM IN YOUR HOUSE...

MOM, FILL OUT THIS SCENARIO

SPARING NO EXPENSE, WHAT WOULD YOU WANT TO USE IT FOR?

....

....

....

....

....

....

HOW WOULD YOU DECORATE IT AND WHAT OTHER THINGS WOULD YOU PUT IN IT?

....

....

....

....

....

....

WOULD YOU SHARE THIS SPACE WITH THE FAMILY?

....

....

....

YOU HAVE AN EMPTY ROOM IN YOUR HOUSE...

DAUGHTER, FILL OUT THIS SCENARIO

SPARING NO EXPENSE, WHAT WOULD YOU WANT TO USE IT FOR?

HOW WOULD YOU DECORATE IT AND WHAT OTHER THINGS WOULD YOU PUT IN IT?

WOULD YOU SHARE THIS SPACE WITH THE FAMILY?

YOU HAVE BEEN GIVEN SUPERPOWERS...

MOM, FILL OUT THIS SCENARIO

☐ DISGUISE	☐ NO DISGUISE

WHAT IS YOUR SUPERPOWER?

WHAT ARE TWO THINGS YOU WANT TO ACHIEVE AS A SUPERHERO?

1.	2.

DESCRIBE OR DRAW YOUR SUPERHERO VEHICLE...

DO YOU TELL YOUR FRIENDS AND FAMILY, OR KEEP IT A SECRET? WHY?

YOU HAVE BEEN GIVEN SUPERPOWERS...

DAUGHTER, FILL OUT THIS SCENARIO

❏ DISGUISE | ❏ NO DISGUISE

WHAT IS YOUR SUPERPOWER?

WHAT ARE TWO THINGS YOU WANT TO ACHIEVE AS A SUPERHERO?

1.

2.

DESCRIBE OR DRAW YOUR SUPERHERO VEHICLE...

DO YOU TELL YOUR FRIENDS AND FAMILY, OR KEEP IT A SECRET? WHY?

YOU CAN GO ANYWHERE ON VACATION...

MOM, FILL OUT THIS SCENARIO

ALL EXPENSES PAID, WHERE WOULD YOU GO?

LIST THREE THINGS YOU WANT TO DO?

1.	2.	3.

WHO DO YOU WANT TO BRING WITH YOU?

HOW LONG WILL THE VACATION LAST?

WHY DID YOU CHOOSE THIS PLACE?

YOU CAN GO ANYWHERE ON VACATION...

DAUGHTER, FILL OUT THIS SCENARIO

ALL EXPENSES PAID, WHERE WOULD YOU GO?

LIST THREE THINGS YOU WANT TO DO?

1.	2.	3.

WHO DO YOU WANT TO BRING WITH YOU?

HOW LONG WILL THE VACATION LAST?

WHY DID YOU CHOOSE THIS PLACE?

Answer These!

Answer these prompted questions.
Feel free to skip around or do them in order.

DISCUSS YOUR ANSWERS AND COMPARE YOUR SIMILARITIES AND DIFFERENCES.

QUESTIONS TO ASK YOUR DAUGHTER...

DAUGHTER, ANSWERS THESE... DATE:

1. WHAT WAS THE FUNNIEST PART OF YOUR WEEK?

2. DID SOMETHING HAPPEN THIS WEEK THAT MADE YOU FEEL SCARED OR ALONE?

3. TELL ME ONE THING THAT MADE YOU FEEL SMART.

4. WHAT IS THE LEAST FAVORITE PART OF YOUR SCHOOL DAY?

5. WHAT IS THE BEST PART ABOUT BEING A KID?

QUESTIONS TO ASK YOUR MOM...

MOM, ANSWERS THESE...DATE:

1. HOW IS SCHOOL DIFFERENT NOW THEN WHEN YOU WENT?

2. WHAT WAS YOUR FAVORITE PART OF YOUR SCHOOL DAY?

3. WHAT WAS IT LIKE BEING MY AGE?

4. IS BEING A MOM HARD?

5. WHAT IS THE BEST PART ABOUT BEING A MOM?

MOM, A LITTLE BIT ABOUT YOU...

WHAT IS THE MOST IMPORTANT THING IN YOUR LIFE RIGHT NOW?

WHAT IS THE FIRST THING PEOPLE NOTICE ABOUT YOU?

THREE THINGS YOU LIKE ABOUT YOUR DAUGHTER...

DAUGHTER, A LITTLE BIT ABOUT YOU...

WHAT IS THE MOST IMPORTANT THING IN YOUR LIFE RIGHT NOW?

WHAT IS THE FIRST THING PEOPLE NOTICE ABOUT YOU?

THREE THINGS YOU LIKE ABOUT YOUR MOM...

MOM, A LITTLE BIT ABOUT YOU...

WHAT ARE THREE THINGS YOU ARE PROUD TO HAVE DONE AS A MOTHER?

_____

_____

_____

_____

_____

_____

WHAT ARE THREE THINGS YOU WOULD LIKE TO IMPROVE ON AS A MOTHER?

_____

_____

_____

_____

_____

WHAT IS SOMETHING YOUR MOTHER DID, THAT YOU DO NOW?

_____

_____

_____

_____

_____

DAUGHTER, A LITTLE BIT ABOUT YOU...

WHAT ARE THREE THINGS YOUR MOTHER DOES FOR YOU THAT MAKES YOU HAPPY?

....

....

....

....

....

....

WHAT ARE THREE THINGS YOU COULD DO BETTER FOR YOUR MOM?

....

....

....

....

....

....

WHAT IS SOMETHING YOU WANT YOUR MOM TO HELP YOU WITH MORE OFTEN?

....

....

....

....

....

....

MOM, A LITTLE BIT ABOUT YOU...

WHAT DO MOST OF YOUR FRIENDS HAVE IN COMMON?

....

....

....

....

....

....

WHO KNOWS YOU BETTER THAN ANYONE ELSE? WHY IS THAT?

....

....

....

....

....

WHAT DO YOU SEE AS A WEAKNESS ABOUT YOU, THAT FRIENDS SAY IS A STRENGTH?

....

....

....

....

....

....

DAUGHTER, A LITTLE BIT ABOUT YOU...

WHAT DO MOST OF YOUR FRIENDS HAVE IN COMMON?

WHO KNOWS YOU BETTER THAN ANYONE ELSE? WHY IS THAT?

DO YOU HAVE CHARACTER FLAWS? WHAT ARE THEY?

MOM, A LITTLE BIT ABOUT YOU...

WHAT IS THE BEST THING YOUR MOM EVER DID FOR YOU?

WHAT IS THE HARDEST THING YOUR MOM EVER DID FOR YOU?

WHO DO YOU TRUST MOST IN YOUR LIFE?

DAUGHTER, A LITTLE BIT ABOUT YOU...

WHAT IS THE BEST THING YOUR MOM EVER DID FOR YOU?

WHAT IS THE HARDEST THING YOUR MOM EVER DID FOR YOU?

WHO DO YOU TRUST MOST IN YOUR LIFE?

MOM, A LITTLE BIT ABOUT YOU...

DO YOU HOLD A GRUDGE? WHY OR WHY NOT?

HAVE YOU HAD A BLESSING IN DISGUISE? WHAT WAS IT?

WHAT IS THE MOST IMPORTANT LESSON YOU HAVE LEARNED AS AN ADULT?

DAUGHTER, A LITTLE BIT ABOUT YOU...

DO YOU HOLD A GRUDGE? WHY OR WHY NOT?

HAVE YOU HAD A BLESSING IN DISGUISE? WHAT WAS IT?

WHAT IS THE MOST IMPORTANT LESSON YOU HAVE LEARNED AS A KID?

MOM, A LITTLE BIT ABOUT YOU...

ONE THING YOUR DAUGHTER DOES THAT YOU APPRECIATE AND WHY?

HAVE YOU EVER MADE SOMEONE CRY? WHAT HAPPENED?

WHAT ARE THREE THINGS THAT ARE MOST IMPORTANT TO YOU WHEN CHOOSING FRIENDS?

DAUGHTER, A LITTLE BIT ABOUT YOU...

ONE THING YOUR MOM DOES THAT YOU APPRECIATE AND WHY?

HAVE YOU EVER MADE SOMEONE CRY? WHAT HAPPENED?

WHAT ARE THREE THINGS THAT ARE MOST IMPORTANT TO YOU WHEN CHOOSING FRIENDS?

MOM, A LITTLE BIT ABOUT YOU...

WHAT IS ONE HABIT YOU HAVE THAT YOU WOULD LIKE TO CHANGE?

WHAT DO YOU LOVE TO EAT THAT MOST PEOPLE THINK IS GROSS?

IF YOU COULD ASK ONE PERSON (DEAD OR ALIVE) ONE QUESTION, WHAT WOULD IT BE?

DAUGHTER, A LITTLE BIT ABOUT YOU...

WHAT IS ONE HABIT YOU HAVE THAT YOU WOULD LIKE TO CHANGE?

WHAT DO YOU LOVE TO EAT THAT MOST PEOPLE THINK IS GROSS?

IF YOU COULD ASK ONE PERSON (DEAD OR ALIVE) ONE QUESTION, WHAT WOULD IT BE?

MOM, A LITTLE BIT ABOUT YOU...

WOULD YOU WANT TO OWN A PRIVATE JET OR LUXURY YACHT? WHY?

WHAT IS THE CRAZIEST THING YOU HAVE ASKED ALEXA OR SIRI?

WHAT 3 THINGS WOULD YOU PUT IN A TIME CAPSULE FOR PEOPLE TO OPEN IN 50 YEARS? WHY?

DAUGHTER, A LITTLE BIT ABOUT YOU...

WOULD YOU WANT TO OWN A PRIVATE JET OR A LUXURY YACHT? WHY

WHAT IS THE CRAZIEST THING YOU HAVE ASKED ALEXA OR SIRI?

WHAT 3 THINGS WOULD YOU PUT IN A TIME CAPSULE FOR PEOPLE TO OPEN IN 50 YEARS? WHY?

MOM, A LITTLE BIT ABOUT YOU...

WHAT WAS YOUR FAVORITE SUBJECT IN SCHOOL? WHY?

WHAT WAS YOUR LEAST FAVORITE SUBJECT IN SCHOOL? WHY?

IF YOU COULD GIVE YOUR PAST SELF ONE PIECE OF ADVICE ABOUT SCHOOL, WHAT WOULD IT BE?

DAUGHTER, A LITTLE BIT ABOUT YOU...

WHAT IS YOUR FAVORITE SUBJECT IN SCHOOL? WHY?

WHAT IS YOUR LEAST FAVORITE SUBJECT IN SCHOOL? WHY?

IF YOU COULD GIVE YOUR PAST SELF ONE PIECE OF ADVICE ABOUT SCHOOL, WHAT WOULD IT BE?

QUESTION FOR MOM...

WHAT WAS IT LIKE GROWING UP WITH YOUR MOM? WHAT WAS SHE LIKE?

_____

_____

_____

_____

_____

_____

_____

_____

_____

WHAT DO YOU ADMIRE ABOUT HER?

_____

_____

_____

_____

_____

_____

_____

_____

QUESTION FOR DAUGHTER...

TELL ME WHAT YOU KNOW AND LIKE ABOUT YOUR GRANDMA (YOUR MOM'S MOM)...

WHAT DO YOU ADMIRE ABOUT HER?

Doodle It!

In this section doodle the objects listed, any way you want! Have fun with it and don't worry if it's not perfect.

WHEN FINISHED, WHAT ARE SOME INTERESTING WAYS YOU BOTH SEE THINGS IN THIS WORLD FROM YOUR DRAWINGS?

DOODLE TIME!

MOM, DRAW EACH OBJECT

BIRD	TREE
DOG	HOUSE

DOODLE TIME!

DAUGHTER, DRAW EACH OBJECT

BIRD	TREE

DOG	HOUSE

DOODLE TIME!

MOM, DRAW EACH OBJECT

SUN	CAT

HORSE	FLOWER

DOODLE TIME!

DAUGHTER, DRAW EACH OBJECT

SUN

CAT

HORSE

FLOWER

DOODLE TIME!

MOM, DRAW EACH OBJECT

AIRPLANE

CAR

BUTTERFLY

SPACESHIP

DOODLE TIME!

DAUGHTER, DRAW EACH OBJECT

AIRPLANE

CAR

BUTTERFLY

SPACESHIP

DOODLE TIME!

MOM, DRAW EACH OBJECT

FISH

CUPCAKE

PALM TREE

ALIEN

DOODLE TIME!

DAUGHTER, DRAW EACH OBJECT

FISH

CUPCAKE

PALM TREE

ALIEN

DOODLE TIME!

MOM, DRAW EACH OBJECT

| BALLOONS | COOKIE |

| SUNSET | MONSTER |

DOODLE TIME!

DAUGHTER, DRAW EACH OBJECT

| BALLOONS | COOKIE |

| SUNSET | MONSTER |

RELAX A BIT AND COLOR THIS PAGE ANYWAY YOU LIKE...

MOM, GET SOMETHING TO COLOR WITH AND COLOR AWAY!

RELAX A BIT AND COLOR THIS PAGE ANYWAY YOU LIKE...

DAUGHTER, GET SOMETHING TO COLOR WITH AND COLOR AWAY!

Ask Some Questions!

In this section create some of your own questions you want answered.

GO OVER YOUR ANSWERS AND DISCUSS.

MOM, ASK A QUESTION FOR YOUR DAUGHTER TO ANSWER...

QUESTION:

ANSWER:

DAUGHTER, ASK A QUESTION FOR YOUR MOM TO ANSWER...

QUESTION:

ANSWER:

MOM, ASK A QUESTION FOR YOUR DAUGHTER TO ANSWER...

QUESTION:

ANSWER:

DAUGHTER, ASK A QUESTION FOR YOUR MOM TO ANSWER...

QUESTION:

ANSWER:

MOM, ASK A QUESTION FOR YOUR DAUGHTER TO ANSWER...

QUESTION:

ANSWER:

DAUGHTER, ASK A QUESTION FOR YOUR MOM TO ANSWER...

QUESTION:

ANSWER:

MOM, ASK A QUESTION FOR YOUR DAUGHTER TO ANSWER...

QUESTION:

ANSWER:

DAUGHTER, ASK A QUESTION FOR YOUR MOM TO ANSWER...

QUESTION:

ANSWER:

MOM, ASK A QUESTION FOR YOUR DAUGHTER TO ANSWER...

QUESTION:

ANSWER:

DAUGHTER, ASK A QUESTION FOR YOUR MOM TO ANSWER...

QUESTION:

ANSWER:

Would You Rather

These are some fun exercises to learn more about how each of you think.

GO OVER YOUR ANSWERS AND SEE WHERE YOU HAVE SIMILARITIES AND DIFFERENCES.

WOULD YOU RATHER...

FOR MOM, WRITE WHICH ONE YOU WOULD RATHER

HAVE A MAGIC CARPET OR PERSONAL ROBOT?

BE THE FUNNIEST PERSON OR SMARTEST PERSON ALIVE?

BE INVISIBLE OR BE ABLE TO FLY?

BE 5 YEARS YOUNGER OR 10 YEARS OLDER?

CONTROL THE WEATHER OR TALK TO ANIMALS?

BE FAMOUS OR RICH?

ALWAYS HAVE TO TELL THE TRUTH OR ALWAYS HAVE TO LIE?

LIVE WITHOUT MOVIES OR WITHOUT MUSIC?

LIVE SOMEWHERE ALWAYS HOT OR ALWAYS COLD?

BE A BIRD OR A FISH?

READ MINDS OR SEE THE FUTURE?

BE ABLE TO TELEPORT YOURSELF ANYWHERE OR TIME TRAVEL?

HAVE SUPER HEARING OR X-RAY VISION?

BE AN ADULT YOUR WHOLE LIFE OR BE A KID YOUR WHOLE LIFE?

HAVE UNLIMITED TIME OR UNLIMITED MONEY?

LIVE IN THE COUNTRY OR LIVE IN THE CITY

BE TOOTHLESS OR BE BALD?

SWIM IN A POOL OF PUDDING OR A POOL IF JELL-O?

HOW MANY DID YOU HAVE THAT WERE THE SAME? TALK ABOUT WHY YOU CHOSE THESE ANSWERS.

WOULD YOU RATHER...

FOR DAUGHTER, WRITE WHICH ONE YOU WOULD RATHER

HAVE A MAGIC CARPET OR PERSONAL ROBOT?

BE THE FUNNIEST PERSON OR SMARTEST PERSON ALIVE?

BE INVISIBLE OR BE ABLE TO FLY?

BE 5 YEARS YOUNGER OR 10 YEARS OLDER?

CONTROL THE WEATHER OR TALK TO ANIMALS?

BE FAMOUS OR RICH?

HAVE A HIGH-PITCHED VOICE OR A SUPER DEEP VOICE?

LIVE WITHOUT MOVIES OR WITHOUT MUSIC?

LIVE SOMEWHERE ALWAYS HOT OR ALWAYS COLD?

BE A BIRD OR A FISH?

READ MINDS OR SEE THE FUTURE?

BE ABLE TO TELEPORT YOURSELF ANYWHERE OR TIME TRAVEL?

HAVE SUPER HEARING OR X-RAY VISION?

BE AN ADULT YOUR WHOLE LIFE OR BE A KID YOUR WHOLE LIFE?

HAVE UNLIMITED TIME OR UNLIMITED MONEY?

LIVE IN THE COUNTRY OR LIVE IN THE CITY

BE TOOTHLESS OR BE BALD?

SWIM IN A POOL OF PUDDING OR A POOL IF JELL-O?

HOW MANY DID YOU HAVE THAT WERE THE SAME? TALK ABOUT WHY YOU CHOSE THESE ANSWERS.

This or That!

In this section are some fun and easy ways to get to know each other.

GO OVER YOUR ANSWERS AND SEE WHERE YOU HAVE SIMILARITIES AND DIFFERENCES.

MOM, CHOOSE THIS OR THAT...

FOOD EDITION

PASTA ☐	☐ PIZZA
CAKE ☐	☐ PIE
BREAKFAST ☐	☐ DINNER
WAFFLES ☐	☐ PANCAKES
CHOCOLATE ☐	☐ VANILLA
FRUIT ☐	☐ VEGETABLES
MILD ☐	☐ HOT
SWEET ☐	☐ SALTY
DINE IN ☐	☐ TAKE OUT
FROZEN YOGURT ☐	☐ ICE CREAM
COKE ☐	☐ PEPSI
TACO ☐	☐ BURRITO
FRENCH FRIES ☐	☐ MASHED POTATOES

HOW MANY ITEMS DID YOU HAVE IN COMMON?

DAUGHTER, CHOOSE THIS OR THAT...

FOOD EDITION

PASTA	☐ ☐	PIZZA
CAKE	☐ ☐	PIE
BREAKFAST	☐ ☐	DINNER
WAFFLES	☐ ☐	PANCAKES
CHOCOLATE	☐ ☐	VANILLA
FRUIT	☐ ☐	VEGETABLES
MILD	☐ ☐	HOT
SWEET	☐ ☐	SALTY
DINE IN	☐ ☐	TAKE OUT
FROZEN YOGURT	☐ ☐	ICE CREAM
COKE	☐ ☐	PEPSI
TACO	☐ ☐	BURRITO
FRENCH FRIES	☐ ☐	MASHED POTATOES

HOW MANY ITEMS DID YOU HAVE IN COMMON?

MOM, CHOOSE THIS OR THAT...

TRAVEL EDITION

BEACH ☐	☐	MOUNTAINS
AIRPLANE ☐	☐	BOAT
CITY ☐	☐	COUNTRY
RELAXING ☐	☐	ADVENTURE
SUMMER ☐	☐	WINTER
HOTEL ☐	☐	AIR BNB
BACKPACK ☐	☐	SUITCASE
GROUP ☐	☐	ALONE
GLAMPING ☐	☐	CAMPING
RESTAURANT ☐	☐	FOOD TRUCK
HAVE A PLAN ☐	☐	GO WITH THE FLOW
SWIM IN THE OCEAN ☐	☐	SWIM IN THE POOL
COOK ☐	☐	EAT OUT

HOW MANY ITEMS DID YOU HAVE IN COMMON?

DAUGHTER, CHOOSE THIS OR THAT...

TRAVEL EDITION

BEACH ☐	☐	MOUNTAINS
AIRPLANE ☐	☐	BOAT
CITY ☐	☐	COUNTRY
RELAXING ☐	☐	ADVENTURE
SUMMER ☐	☐	WINTER
HOTEL ☐	☐	AIR BNB
BACKPACK ☐	☐	SUITCASE
GROUP ☐	☐	ALONE
GLAMPING ☐	☐	CAMPING
RESTAURANT ☐	☐	FOOD TRUCK
HAVE A PLAN ☐	☐	GO WITH THE FLOW
SWIM IN THE OCEAN ☐	☐	SWIM IN THE POOL
COOK ☐	☐	EAT OUT

HOW MANY ITEMS DID YOU HAVE IN COMMON?

MOM, CHOOSE THIS OR THAT...

ABOUT YOU EDITION

CAT	☐	☐	DOG
READING	☐	☐	AUDIO BOOK
INTROVERT	☐	☐	EXTROVERT
EARLY BIRD	☐	☐	NIGHT OWL
BEING HOT	☐	☐	BEING COLD
YOUTUBE	☐	☐	NETFLIX
LEFTY	☐	☐	RIGHTY
VINTAGE	☐	☐	MODERN
BATH	☐	☐	SHOWER
OUTSIDE	☐	☐	INSIDE
TEXT	☐	☐	CALL
TV	☐	☐	MOVIE
COMEDY	☐	☐	DRAMA

HOW MANY ITEMS DID YOU HAVE IN COMMON?

DAUGHTER, CHOOSE THIS OR THAT...

ABOUT YOU EDITION

CAT ☐	☐	DOG
READING ☐	☐	AUDIO BOOK
INTROVERT ☐	☐	EXTROVERT
EARLY BIRD ☐	☐	NIGHT OWL
BEING HOT ☐	☐	BEING COLD
YOUTUBE ☐	☐	TIKTOK
LEFTY ☐	☐	RIGHTY
VINTAGE ☐	☐	MODERN
BATH ☐	☐	SHOWER
OUTSIDE ☐	☐	INSIDE
TEXT ☐	☐	CALL
TV ☐	☐	MOVIE
COMEDY ☐	☐	DRAMA

HOW MANY ITEMS DID YOU HAVE IN COMMON?

Activities!

Getting up and moving around is important for everyone. Let's get some blood flowing and do a few activities together

HOW CAN YOU INCORPORATE DAILY ACTIVITIES YOU BOTH CAN DO A FEW TIMES A WEEK TOGETHER?

LET'S TIE-DYE!

Tie-dye Materials Needed

(YOU CAN ALSO LOOK UP DYE KITS THAT WILL HAVE SOME OF THESE ITEMS INCLUDED TOGETHER)

WHITE, 100% COTTON ITEM	❑	GALLON-SIZED ZIP PLASTIC BAGS	❑
SEVERAL COLORS OF DYE	❑	WATER FOR INK BOTTLES	❑
SQUIRT BOTTLES (ONE FOR EACH COLOR)	❑	A SPRAY BOTTLE OF WATER	❑
RUBBER BANDS	❑	PAPER TOWELS OR RAGS FOR SPILLS	❑
RUBBER GLOVES	❑		

Project Preparation

- **SET UP** For a new apparel item, machine wash & dry first, but don't use fabric softener or a dryer sheet. This could leave a residue on the fabric that could repel the ink. Cover your workspace with a plastic tablecloth (or set up outside).

- **PREPARE THE INK** If you bought a kit, set up the ink in the bottles according to the tie-dye instructions. If you bought powered or liquid dye, prepare it according to package instructions & put the ink into the squirt bottles.

- **PREPARE THE APPAREL ITEM** Spray with water to dampen, search online for Tie-Dye patterns you like best to try or produce your own. Twist & use rubber bands to secure it in your pattern.

- **INKING THE ITEM** Squeeze ink onto the sections per kit instructions or per the pattern you've decided to follow — or freestyle it! Once finished dying, place each shirt in a sealed plastic bag for 24 hours to allow ink to set & the colors to become vibrant.

- **RINSE** After 24 hours, put on rubber gloves, remove from the bag & rinse it in cold water (without removing the rubber bands) until the water runs clear of the dye. Then remove the rubber bands, rinse again, then machine wash and dry on the hottest setting allowed on the tag. Do not combine with any other clothing for that initial wash & dry in case any dye bleeds. When it's dry, it's ready to wear.

LET'S GO ON A SCAVENGER HUNT...

GET OUTSIDE AND GO ON A **NATURE** SCAVENGER HUNT!

- ❑ GREEN LEAF
- ❑ BROWN LEAF
- ❑ PINECONE
- ❑ SOMETHING BLACK
- ❑ SOMETHING GREY
- ❑ SOMETHING RED
- ❑ FEATHER
- ❑ WEEDS
- ❑ SMOOTH ROCK
- ❑ STICK
- ❑ BIRDS NEST
- ❑ FEATHER
- ❑ FLYING BIRD
- ❑ WATER
- ❑ SPIDERWEB

- ❑ BUTTERFLY
- ❑ AIRPLANE
- ❑ TALL GRASS
- ❑ CUT GRASS
- ❑ GRASSHOPPER
- ❑ ANT
- ❑ MOSS
- ❑ TREE BARK
- ❑ ROUGH ROCK
- ❑ BUG
- ❑ WHITE FLOWER
- ❑ YELLOW FLOWER
- ❑ SOMETHING ROUND
- ❑ MUD
- ❑ FRUIT TREE

HOW MANY ITEMS DID YOU FIND?

LET'S GO ON A SCAVENGER HUNT...

STAY INSIDE AND GO ON AN **INDOOR** SCAVENGER HUNT!

- ☐ SOMETHING SOFT
- ☐ A STAR
- ☐ SOMETHING OPEN
- ☐ SOMETHING SPARKLY
- ☐ SOMETHING STRETCHY
- ☐ A BUTTON
- ☐ SCARF
- ☐ THIN BOOK
- ☐ BIG BOOK
- ☐ SOMETHING SQUARE
- ☐ SOMETHING ROUND
- ☐ SOMETHING RECTANGLE
- ☐ SOMETHING THAT MAKES NOISE
- ☐ BATTERY
- ☐ SOMETHING PURPLE

- ☐ SOMETHING GREEN
- ☐ SOMETHING BROWN
- ☐ SOMETHING CLOSED
- ☐ SOMETHING CLEAR
- ☐ A TISSUE
- ☐ SOMETHING ON WHEELS
- ☐ HAT
- ☐ BALL
- ☐ SOMETHING WITH THE LETTER V
- ☐ SOMETHING WITH THE LETTER C
- ☐ PENCIL
- ☐ SUNGLASSES
- ☐ CHAPSTICK
- ☐ CANDLE
- ☐ FLASHLIGHT

HOW MANY ITEMS DID YOU FIND?

LET'S GO ON A SCAVENGER HUNT...

MAKE UP YOUR OWN!

- [ ]
- [ ]
- [ ]
- [ ]
- [ ]
- [ ]
- [ ]
- [ ]
- [ ]
- [ ]
- [ ]
- [ ]
- [ ]
- [ ]
- [ ]

- [ ]
- [ ]
- [ ]
- [ ]
- [ ]
- [ ]
- [ ]
- [ ]
- [ ]
- [ ]
- [ ]
- [ ]
- [ ]
- [ ]
- [ ]

HOW MANY ITEMS DID YOU FIND?

LET'S GO ON A SCAVENGER HUNT...

MAKE UP YOUR OWN!

- ☐ ....
- ☐ ....
- ☐ ....
- ☐ ....
- ☐ ....
- ☐ ....
- ☐ ....
- ☐ ....
- ☐ ....
- ☐ ....
- ☐ ....
- ☐ ....
- ☐ ....
- ☐ ....
- ☐

- ☐ ....
- ☐ ....
- ☐ ....
- ☐ ....
- ☐ ....
- ☐ ....
- ☐ ....
- ☐ ....
- ☐ ....
- ☐ ....
- ☐ ....
- ☐ ....
- ☐ ....
- ☐ ....
- ☐

HOW MANY ITEMS DID YOU FIND?

Things To Do

In this section write a bucket list and things you would like to do together

DISCUSS WHAT YOU HAVE WRITTEN DOWN AND MAYBE SET SOME PLANS TO CROSS SOME OF THESE OFF YOUR LIST!

CREATE A BUCKET LIST...

FOR MOM, WRITE DOWN EVERYTHING YOU
WOULD LIKE TO DO ON THIS EARTH.

- ☐
- ☐
- ☐
- ☐
- ☐
- ☐
- ☐
- ☐
- ☐
- ☐
- ☐
- ☐
- ☐
- ☐
- ☐
- ☐
- ☐
- ☐
- ☐

CREATE A BUCKET LIST...

FOR DAUGHTER, WRITE DOWN EVERYTHING YOU WOULD LIKE TO DO ON THIS EARTH.

- ☐
- ☐
- ☐
- ☐
- ☐
- ☐
- ☐
- ☐
- ☐
- ☐
- ☐
- ☐
- ☐
- ☐
- ☐
- ☐
- ☐
- ☐

THINGS YOU CAN DO TOGETHER...

FOR MOM: WRITE DOWN THINGS YOU CAN DO TOGETHER

ACTIVITIES

- ☐
- ☐
- ☐
- ☐
- ☐
- ☐

GAMES

- ☐
- ☐
- ☐
- ☐
- ☐
- ☐

TRAVELS

- ☐
- ☐
- ☐
- ☐
- ☐
- ☐

THINGS YOU CAN DO TOGETHER...

FOR DAUGHTER: WRITE DOWN THINGS YOU WANT TO DO TOGETHER

ACTIVITIES

- [ ]
- [ ]
- [ ]
- [ ]
- [ ]
- [ ]

GAMES

- [ ]
- [ ]
- [ ]
- [ ]
- [ ]
- [ ]

TRAVELS

- [ ]
- [ ]
- [ ]
- [ ]
- [ ]
- [ ]

Story Time

In this section each of you create a character and tell a short story of an adventure they go on.

READ EACH OTHERS STORY AND TALK ABOUT WHAT THEIR ADVENTURES WERE.

MOM, LET'S CREATE A STORY CHARACTER...

CIRCLE ONE, IS YOUR CHARACTER A...

HUMAN   OR   ANIMAL

Info & Appearance

WHAT IS YOUR CHARACTERS FULL NAME?		IF AN ANIMAL WHICH TYPE OF ANIMAL?	
HOW OLD ARE THEY?	EYE COLOR?	HAIR COLOR?	GLASSES?
FRECKLES?	TALL OR SHORT?	BODY TYPE?	HE OR SHE?

OTHER CHARACTERISTICS YOU WANT TO ADD?

....

....

Characters Favorites

COLOR?	MUSIC?	FOOD?	HOBBIES?

OTHER FAVORITES OR DISLIKES YOU WANT TO ADD?

....

....

Character Family and Friends

PARENT NAME?			PARENT NAME?	
OTHER FAMILY? FILL OUT BOXES			SIBLINGS?	SIBLING NAME(S)?
			SIBLING AGES?	OTHER SIBLING INFO?

BEST FRIENDS NAME?

ANIMAL OR HUMAN? IF AN ANIMAL, WHAT KIND?

WHAT DO THEY LIKE TO DO TOGETHER?

OTHER FRIENDS?

Personality Traits

INTROVERT	❏	❏	EXTROVERT
LOGICAL	❏	❏	EMOTIONAL
BOOK-SMART	❏	❏	STREET SMART
OPTIMISTIC	❏	❏	PESSIMISTIC
ORGANIZED	❏	❏	MESSY
CALM	❏	❏	EXCITABLE
AFFECTIONATE	❏	❏	RESERVED
BOLD	❏	❏	CAUTIOUS
FUN	❏	❏	SCARED-Y CAT

MOM, LET'S CREATE A STORY CHARACTER...

IF YOU WANT, DRAW YOUR MAIN CHARACTER AND ANY OTHER
CHARACTERS THAT ARE IMPORTANT IN YOUR STORY.

STORY OUTLINE...

Your characters are going on an adventure!

THEY ARE GOING ON AN ADVENTURE TO FIND LOST GEMS...

WHAT IS YOUR MAIN CHARACTER'S ROLE IN THE STORY?

WHO ELSE IS GOING? WHAT IS THEIR ROLES IN THE ADVENTURE?

WHERE DO THEY HAVE TO TRAVEL TO, TO FIND THE TREASURE?

WHAT IS THE TREASURE?
DRAW OR DESCRIBE IT.

LET'S WRITE YOUR STORY...

Tell a short story about your adventure...

TAKE YOUR TIME, YOU DON'T HAVE TO DO IT ONE SITTING.

LET'S WRITE YOUR STORY...

Story continued...(if you need more room)

DAUGHTER, LET'S CREATE A STORY CHARACTER...

CIRCLE ONE, IS YOUR CHARACTER A...

HUMAN OR ANIMAL

Info & Appearance

WHAT IS YOUR CHARACTERS FULL NAME?		IF AN ANIMAL WHICH TYPE OF ANIMAL?	
HOW OLD ARE THEY?	EYE COLOR?	HAIR COLOR?	GLASSES?
FRECKLES?	TALL OR SHORT?	BODY TYPE?	HE OR SHE?

OTHER CHARACTERISTICS YOU WANT TO ADD?

Characters Favorites

COLOR?	MUSIC?	FOOD?	HOBBIES?

OTHER FAVORITES OR DISLIKES YOU WANT TO ADD?

Character Family and Friends

PARENT NAME?		PARENT NAME?	
OTHER FAMILY? FILL OUT BOXES		SIBLINGS?	SIBLING NAME(S)?
		SIBLING AGES?	OTHER SIBLING INFO?

BEST FRIENDS NAME?

ANIMAL OR HUMAN? IF AN ANIMAL, WHAT KIND?

WHAT DO THEY LIKE TO DO TOGETHER?

OTHER FRIENDS?

Personality Traits

INTROVERT	❑	❑	EXTROVERT
LOGICAL	❑	❑	EMOTIONAL
BOOK-SMART	❑	❑	STREET SMART
OPTIMISTIC	❑	❑	PESSIMISTIC
ORGANIZED	❑	❑	MESSY
CALM	❑	❑	EXCITABLE
AFFECTIONATE	❑	❑	RESERVED
BOLD	❑	❑	CAUTIOUS
FUN	❑	❑	SCARED-Y CAT

DAUGHTER, LET'S CREATE A STORY CHARACTER...

IF YOU WANT DRAW YOUR MAIN CHARACTER AND ANY OTHER
CHARACTERS THAT ARE IMPORTANT IN YOUR STORY.

STORY OUTLINE...

Your characters are going on an adventure!

THEY ARE GOING TO FIND A HIDDEN TREASURE...

WHAT IS YOUR MAIN CHARACTER'S ROLE IN THE STORY?

WHO ELSE GOING? WHAT ARE THEIR ROLES IN THE ADVENTURE?

WHERE DO THEY HAVE TO TRAVEL TO, TO FIND THE TREASURE?

WHAT IS THE TREASURE?
DRAW OR DESCRIBE IT.

LET'S WRITE YOUR STORY...

Tell a short story about your adventure...

TAKE YOUR TIME, YOU DON'T HAVE TO DO IT ONE SITTING.

LET'S WRITE YOUR STORY...

Story continued...(if you need more room)